# INDIO TRAILS

## A XICANO ODYSSEY
## THROUGH
## INDIAN COUNTRY

Other books by raúlrsalinas:

*Viaje / Trip*
(1973)

*Un Trip through the Mind Jail*
*y otras Excursions*
(1980, new edition 2002)

*East of the Freeway*
(1996)


Audio recordings:

*Los Many Mundos of raúlrsalinas*
(2000)

*Beyond the Beaten Path*
(2002)

*Red Arc: A call for liberación con salsa y cool*
(2005)

# INDIO TRAILS

## A XICANO ODYSSEY
## THROUGH
## INDIAN COUNTRY

by

raúlrsalinas
(Autumn Sun)

*San Antonio, Tejas*
*2007*

Cover photo, by Bryce Milligan, shows a 1,000-year-old
pictograph image of a shaman located in Panther Cave,
Seminole Canyon, Texas.

First Edition

ISBN-10: 0-916727-37-8 (paperback original)
ISBN-13: 978-0-916727-37-6

Wings Press
627 E. Guenther • San Antonio, Texas 78210
Phone/fax: (210) 271-7805

On-line catalogue and ordering: www.wingspress.com

Library of Congress Cataloging-in-Publication Data

Raúlrsalinas, 1934-
  Indio trails : a Xicano odyssey through Indian country / by
Raúlrsalinas (Autumn Sun) ; with an introduction by Louis Mendoza.
-- 1st ed.
    p. cm.
  ISBN-13: 978-0-916727-37-6 (alk. paper)
  ISBN-10: 0-916727-37-8 (alk. paper)
  1. Indians of North America--Poetry.  I. Mendoza, Louis Gerard,
1960- II. Title.
  PS3568.A82I63 2006
  811'.54--dc22
                                    2006017510

Grateful acknowledgement to the following publications where the fol-
lowing poems appeared: "Unity Vision," "Forest/Desert Vision,"
"Love/War," "Survival Song," and "Prayer for a Newborn" first
appeared in *Un Trip through the Mind Jail* (San Francisco: Ediciones
Pocho che, 1st edition, 1980). "About Invasion" and "Conquest" first
appeared in *East of the Freeway* (Austin: Red Salmon Press, 1996).
"Conversation at a Greyhound Bus Depot" and "Combat Vision" first
appeared in *Cipactli Review (*San Francisco State Univ., 2001).
"Offering to Marsha" first appeared in Spanish as "Ofrenda 'pa
Marsha" in *Calaca* and in *La Peña newsletter*.

# CONTENTS

*To those who forged the path before us;*
*to those who showed me the way;*
*and for the children.*

# Author's Preface

Now it is done – the circle is complete; and so is this collection of writings, both of which were so difficult and painful to finalize. (No beat generation road trip, here – but a trip, nonetheless.) Upon my release from the cages of Marion's control unit, naïve, impressionable and ready to be of service to the movement, I began to document my life in exile in Washington State. After a two year long period involved in the reclamation and takeover of land with El Centro de La Raza, I was introduced to the native peoples of the region. Most of these poems were born from scribblings documenting their causes, which became my causes. Culture in the schools, Northwest AIM ceremonies with Joe Washington. Learning on the river, we faced the feds, the yearly floods at Frank's Landing, the Olympia-to-Portland march (after the June 25th thing in Oglala). Others were scratched out during short intervals of breathing space, mapping out the then-as-yet-uncharted Trail of Self-Determination, blowing on those buy-centennial blues. Family life in Suquamish, my bros-in-law, the George boys, Chacon's bust in Mejico kept us quite busy, as did the shootout in Vail, Oregon (which also tied us up muchly!). The takeover of the cascadia juvenile jail, that later became the Chief Leschi Medical Building; the restructuring of people's politics and heads. The repression intensified, and so did the struggle. Then came the trials: Custer, Vancouver, Cedar Rapids, Fargo, L.A., Milwaukee. International relations, Las Américas, europa. El Rio Escondido with Roxanne, Panama with the Kuna youth. Soon the journey began to get ugly, the external forces were mounting as we moved inward, taking

wrong turns, stumbling, paranoia & reprisals, making
mistakes, and it just got harder to sit and think of round-
ing out a manuscript. Living with the memory of those no
longer with us: Valerie, who went with the river defend-
ing her nets; Loren & Roque who also went the way of the
salmon; Bill Wahpepah & the crew storming the nuclear
plant in Dodewaard, dinner guests of North African
colonels; Ingrid in Genève (later gunned down by rene-
gades of the FARC in Colombia); Ana Mae (gunned down
by renegades over here). What to reveal, what not to say?
Nilak's body (and ours) invaded by foreign illnesses: car-
cinoma clouds the lungs, cirrhosis (bad livers from bad
living). So, with the departure of Frances, she who bore
me, and the passing of my comrade Steve Robideau, who
accompanied me on most of this jaunt, I give blessings to
Bryce Milligan for patience & beyond, shoutouts & props
to Rene and Gabi, my work partners for cutting through
the rant and the rave, it is time to bring ths beat-up book-
let to a close.

Love in Struggle,

Autumn Sun
raúlrsalinas

x

# Peregrinations
# of a Xicanindio Poet

The publication of *Indio Trails: A Xicano Odyssey Through Indian Country* is long overdue, having incubated for three decades within the poet's portfolio of unpublished writings. Though some of these poems have appeared in other contexts, most are new to the printed page. More importantly, this collection offers us a unique opportunity to view for the first time a comprehensive collection of Salinas' poems about his years of living and working in solidarity with Native peoples of the Americas.

Readers familiar with Salinas' poetry and political work already know that his life's journey has been one of constant exploration and transformation, a journey that, among other moments of *conscientizaçao*, included a new awareness that as a Chicano his history and destiny are intertwined with that of American Indians. For him, however, this was never a moment for solipsistic self-indulgence, but a call to action, an obligation that required him to integrate two identities he had been taught to think of as distinct from one another. The result was a Xicanindio perspective that charted a path for his politics and his poetry. *Indio Trails* documents a small but significant portion of that journey.

Unable to return home to Texas or California due to parole restrictions, when Salinas gained his release from Marion Prison in November of 1972, he chose to be exiled in Seattle because he had built alliances with students and faculty at the University of Washington. Immediately following his arrival, he joined a multiracial, Latino-led coalition of community groups intent on assuming control of an abandoned school building. Successful in their effort, they formed El Centro de La Raza.

As an activist, student, and instructor, Salinas immersed himself in the Native American fishing rights struggle in the Seattle-Tacoma region, working with the Nisqually/Puyallup peoples. After attending school for three years, he began working full-time at El Centro de La Raza. It was here that his international vision and his ideas regarding Indian-Chicano unity were finely honed. As a staff member of El Centro's Indian-Chicano Education Project, in 1975 he met and worked with AIM member Leonard Peltier. Though not in the forefront of AIM's battles on the Pine Ridge reservation in 1975, Salinas provided tactical support from Seattle. In 1976 he was co-coordinator of the Trail of Self-Determination, a seven-month cross-country educational caravan led by the Survival of American Indians Association, whose purpose was to offer an alternative perspective on the U.S. bicentennial. They arrived in D.C. on July 4 of that year. In 1977 Salinas co-founded the National Leonard Peltier Defense Committee. Four years later he would be selected as part of an International Indian Treaty Council delegation sent to represent Peltier at a Human Rights Symposium in Geneva. Over the years, he has traveled extensively on behalf of the Treaty Council to *intercambios* in Nicaragua, Libya, Puerto Rico, and Mexico.

The poems in *Indio Trails* are centrally, but not exclusively, concerned with this period, the heyday of the American Indian movement from the mid-1970s to the mid-1980s. They thus serve to offer readers an insider's view of this important period of reclamation and resistance. Of equal significance is the poetic mapping of experience that is achieved with this collection. In these poems we see yet another vein of Salinas' incredibly diverse poetics emerge that any single poem or samplings of poems previously published could not possibly express. The collection as a whole takes the reader on a complex journey that is simultaneously geographical, social, political, emotional, cultural, and spiritual in nature.

Beginning with a poem about the refusal to be drawn into the inane discussion about the authenticity of Mexicanos' indigenous identity, the poems offer readers a series of experiences and visions about the process of reclamation and struggle that being Xicanindio entails. More importantly perhaps, the poems teach us the true nature of solidarity as a communion of mind, body, and spirit in concordance with something larger than our individual selves. While there is a strong autobiographical element to many of the poems, we are taken on a journey that proceeds from the Northwest where fishing rights struggles are ongoing to the seat of corrupt government power in Washington, D.C. and back, a trip that along the way covers many of life's terrains: the urban and the rural, the individual and the collective, the personal and the political, as well as the chasm between war and peace, hostility and love, and ignorance and awareness.

This collection is not a blueprint for how this journey can be made, for there can be no such detailed guidebook. Rather, these poetic lines are paeans, chants, prayers, lyrics, tributes, lamentations, and songs made up of heart and spirit borne in relation to others and forged by shared experience. As readers we are witnesses to the profound possibilities, and we are richer for it. As the poet shares with us in "Feel Good Song," knowledge is power, and with it comes responsibility. Awareness of that is only the beginning of our own journey for a more just world:

> Live and learn.
> Live and teach
> Live to know
> Live to give
> Knowledge is beginning.

> – Louis G. Mendoza
> Department of Chicano Studies
> University of Minnesota

Professor Mendoza is the editor of Salinas' selected journalism and correspondence: *raúlrsalinas and the Jail Machine: My Weapon Is My Pen* (University of Texas Press, 2006)

# INDIO TRAILS

## Conversation in a Greyhound
## Bus Depot Coffee Shop

*somewhere West of the Pecos*


"Say buddy are yew a injun?"
"Yeah, man."
"Whut kind?"
"MEXICAN".
"O, ah thot yew wuz a real injun."

As he proceeded to tell me
(quite boringly)
about his 1/64$^{th}$ blood quantum
and his Cherokee PRINCESS grandmother;

my prison-like coffee was getting cold,
the bus was pulling out...
and
    it
      was
        time
          to go!


*Sheffield, Texas*
*on the road to Montana*
*summer 1996*

# On Being / Becoming

Salmon eye
gift for the guests
delicacy for the gods
Dip in Tacuba's
glacier blood
knowing
Nisqually was a chief
Sacred ceremony
INIPI
Sage smudgings
by the river's bank
Dog Soldier duties
diversionary ways
Walk
move in harmony
encampments
caution
corrupt councilors
surround the fort
welcome warrior women
from Cedar People
lands
feasting with folks
S'Klallam/Suquamish
break from the South
reject 200 years
HIStory
CARAVAN
takes to the trail eastward HO!
Face "great white father"
insulting the spirit
o' 76.

Dress down the deer
sack up the clams
substance/survival
bad medicine hits the rez
splits the sheets
Leave how you arrive
soar the sound
bound by tradition
found one day/nights
around sacred fire
holy cactus hosts
voicing vows
COMMITMENT
creature caught
Trapped
rage in the cage
calendar pages collected
"combinate the combination"
"revelations in the revolution"
"university of the universe"
free the Eagle/Man
purify with snow
touch of the turtle
spirit in rebellion
visions of victory
Naming ceremonies
Looking Eagle
be watchful
Naming ceremonies
Autumn Sun
speak to many nations
for red Nations
walk in Eastern Woodlands
dance in the desert
bathe in the bay
Return South

SHARE
giving is receiving
represent
the creatures in the cage
cross the ocean
cold continent
designated duties
travel to the center
close to the source
matrix meetings
support
self-determination
sovereignty
autonomy
liberation
weather the storm.

## Unity Vision

Brief/respiteful
      precious (in the movement) cruise
         down desolate
1st & Spokane streets
      EVOKES
smoke-signals of past
    Seattle springtime struggles
      sad summer
         of Native tragedies
            & Dallas Chicanito deaths.
From empty (wasting) warehouse rows
   a fleeting, darting, silent
      (momentary)
         SONG FOR SANTOS . . .
         . . . BLUES FOR WOUNDED KNEE.
The haunting humming of an Autumn wind
      decries historical lies
         atrocious repetitions of blood.
The Trail
      (almost to no avail)
         of Broken Treaties,
resulting in more broken promises
               and rights
               and minds
               and souls
               and laws ...
those flaws from the claws
         of a predator society
            seeking satiation
inside indigenous heart of earth.

Birth-rights bombarded/
           discarded life of
                      innocent lamb-child
                      SANTOS.
Warrior Drums
           (that speak of hope)
are sounding
           pounding out
an angry call-to-arms.
Staccatoing
           super-sophisticated
weaponry of war
           implodes/EXPLODES
and Pedro Bissonette
           lies dead
Peace loving/war hating Bissonette
           BISON
                      (human replica)
slaughtered
           in the Indian People's fight.
While
           Armored Personnel Carriers
                      (murdering mammoths)
draw the line of demarcation
           the nation of the Sioux
                      begins (again) to rise.
Wise South Dakota
           medicine man
smokes the pipe of peace
           & fans the fires of
                      self-determination
Lakota people seeking liberation
           demanding to be free.


                           *1975*
                           *Indio-Chicano  Unity Carvan*

## Forest / Desert Vision

Far
    from Northwestern
firs & forests,
away
    from mountain peaks
of snow which now glow
in the distance;
past
    vast populations
of western redlands
ancient, ancestral sequoias,
is the isle of Alcatraz
    where some of it
        (without a doubt)
            began.
San Francisco
    where we learn
        that Sandino
is very much alive!
The Gypsy Woman also lives
engaging street-corner sages
in cataclysmic conversations
promising to remember the warriors
    in her leaves of tea.
Freeway is the new way (?)
    bad way to travel to L.A.
Monterrey Peninsula
natural muralistic panorama
backdrop props
    as
Salinas Valley

            stoically lives down
steinbeck reactionary romanticism
of still real lettuce-picking campesino/
mission indio stark realities.

And
        SOLEDAD
            that mad-mutant monster
robber of youth full years
        where tears & fears
                gave way to
Piscean passion
    in poetic
& political eruptions,
hunkers still hungering & sleepy yet
subsisting on
        convicted cadavers
                of the classless set.
While crop-dusting plane
bane of all who till the soil
spoils (almost) clouding
        positive sign
                of high-flying eagle
nearing Red Wind (Chémo's camp)
knowing we can't afford to stop.

3 times
        the eagle has appeared.
First, in Oregon – after that Portland rally/march
– documented as a good symbol/omen by traditional
octogenarian
        Granny Hillaire
of lush Suquamish   S'Klallam ground.
Instantaneous thoughts
        of Southwestern sand paintings
that await us

and the Red Sister of the North
       who carves out her/our lives
in totemistic miniatures.

This time the ($2^{nd}$ one around)
it soars over
meadow-filled Murrieta land
and San Miguel
of infamous 1800's
indio iron/fire brandings.


After the eagle
       came Chémo.
masterful merger
of blossoming human being
       communions.

CHÉMO
       grandfather of
              EL TECOLOTL
                     DE
              TESUQUE PUEBLO
                     C/S


CHÉMO
       who bid us to
"go South, for all is well,
and it is safe to journey."


Downtown L.A.
       polluted parcel of earth
where buffaloes (both red and brown)
       no longer roam,
banished, practically vanished
(genocidal extinction)
from their home.

The third time was in Tejas
        after spirit session
with Andrés,
maestro conchero
capitán general
of Mexica traditions
(who, also aware of the warmongers)
said:
"things will be right,
    in the valley of the sacred roots,
when you arrive."

*Indio-Chicano Unity Caravan*
*September '75*

# Tree of Life Vision

Silver salmon
      bronze medallions
southwardly sojourn
  to the indian territory
      & flutes of bamboo.
Tierra Amarilla
  ("yellow earth")
      villagers
remember (never forgetting)
      spanish (?) land grants
            (never quite regaining)
maintain militant discussions
      in secret
of strategies & measures
      now deemed necessary to survive.
San Antonio
      of
Westside tar(paper)shack
      plastic Holiday Inn
            cradle contradictions.
Where poetic umbilical cord
      lies buried
           on
South Alamo Street
      alleyway
since the dwindling
      days of Depression;
& still
      (at will)
the wicked webs
      of WAR(mongers)

continue to be woven/spun
running risks
        safeguarding
northern/southern
        native
RIGHTS
        &
predominant populace
        (of color)
communicate
        in
gestures, hand signs
        spirit tongues.
South Texas
        trembles
w/ resistance of
        grapefruit/melon pickers
to rightwing redneck
neo-vigilante
posse comitatus
attacks.
Encouraged
        nomadic mestizos
eagerly respond
        after
earlier purging
of evil spirits
in Upper valley
popeye lands.
Magic valley of
        tragic life-death
migrant existence;
of
  farmworker
fisherpeople
        (class)

struggles
        concretely
uniting as ONE.
Surprises!
        for the
Pisces of Peralta:
Sandino lives
in Mercedes
as in the Mission.
Cesar Augusto Chacon
hits hot.

*Indio-Chicano Unity Caravan*
*Sept. 16, '75*

# Combat Vision

*For LP & DJB, 2 native comrades
driven by force to go underground*

The reality of (inevitably) impending
WAR
startles those who once chose
to think it all a game.
There were others/brothers
sisters in the battle
    taking on more serious demeanor
assume graver assignments
as per dictums of the
                    MASS.
The hunted – out of dire necessity –
today become the hunters
at this point of no return.

Burning paths of government wrath
warriors find sanctuary
Northwest country owl's nest
universal sounds & infinite games of chance.
Dancing, the elusive Elk deceives
for one more Sun 'n' Moon
capricious captors
predators.
Indian Hillside motor inn
mockingly teeming with feds
obscenely obscures
Umatilla/Warm Springs
winterlands
unraped (as of yet)

sections of earth
birthplaces of natural land patterns
scarlet sunset splash
the moon illuminates the mountains
cloaking them in mauve.

Waiting for word from ana mae & kamook
a momentary release
wrought thoughts:
fry bread, bone games,
Canadian geese in proud formation
headed South.
And still they're all around/
the jackals who'd devour us;
their fetid smell hangs in the air
Paranoia like the plague
also hovers in the wind.
Time/Energy
wasteful expenditures
spent venting and
and posing
imposingly unspoken queries
of one and our own:
Is it him?
Is it her?
Is it you?
Is it me?

*Vail, Oregon*
*Winter 1975*

# Sisterhood struggle

Clandestine conversations
amid Northwest Territories
"heat"
Dog Soldier Societies
reconnoiter
yankee doodle iron horse
in middle class disguise
while in the course
of wisely stressing sovereignty.

Two women, of Raza/Miq-Maq
first beginnings
sharing valued moments:
their love for Che,
braiding hair with pride,
firearms expertise
and mutual concerns
for what we would leave
for the generations
to come.

*"Going under"*
*Somewhere in the Northwest*
*Late 1975*

# Love / War

*(a metamophosis of sorts)*

A
hazy/lazy
(half-hidden)
Harvest Moon
hung low/
glowing on
two
(new) lovers.
Slightly obscure
October Moon
chamelon moon
of changing seasons
entices lovers
to exchange warm smiles
tenderly touch hands
gripping each other firmly ...
A
  long,
      last,
final kiss
to ease the (burning)
            yearning
before turning
(in accordance with the struggle)
         into
flaming arrow
        &
obsidian axe.

*Berkeley/S.F.*
*Oct. '75*

# Xmas Gift

*(in form of a response)*

*for Georgia*


You ask, if I'll still love you
when I've gone completely mad?
YES!
At that precise moment
when sanity's trap-door springs
& wings of madness carry you/me
and Lenin's *What is to be Done*
into infinitesimal heights;
There, in some blazing
bedlam of the world, I'll make love to you
on beds of jagged nerves
(remembering nights of coral, silver & turquoise)
and read my books to you with mutilated mental eyes
recalling earlier awakenings.
Will I still love you
on the rez/the urban jungle
from some foxhole, trench, or open field???
Yes!
Yes!
and once again,
to reassure you,
YES!!!


*Suquamish*
*December 1976*

# To A Long-Time Comrade

*(by way of criticism)*

*for R.M.*

To praise
the sacred salmon
and make mockery
of the common clam,
in the Indian people's fight
for fishing rights,
is a major
    political
       contra
          diction!

*Suquamish, Washington*
*1976*

21

# Trail of Self-Determination

*(fragments from an attempted journal)*


At Fort Laramie
our first encampment
whistling morning winds
wake up call to swirling straw
of tipi floor.

Dared bitter cold
warm cups of coffee...full of sand!
Heating amerindian flesh & bones
spirits chilled
by those who prowl perimeter
with transfixed eyes 'n' ears
on delegation headed East.

Water Birds
in Winnebago
unfurl banners
before panoramas
once vague & obscure
insuring/unifying
Georgia, Sid & wa'hu
visions
of a trail as yet complete.

The Omaha sang songs
of green moonbeams
proper send-off
to Pottowatomie prairie band
who welcome us
with Thunder Rocks.

Late Summer
southward bound
rounding out last days
"end of the trail"
we load up the yellow school bus
& old ford relic van
pit stops to make:
Lame Deer
returning Northern Cheyenne people safe.

Then up to Fort Peck
Assiniboine country
Woody Kipp,
Myrna Small Salmon and her clan
Gene Heavy Runner of Missoula
or Browning, farewells to the guys
from Rocky Boy.
As we conclude our mission,
stealthily the moon creeps
over cascades as far off in the horizon
the sun makes its descent
into the heart of dusky
Olympic mountain range.
Strange feelings as we move
in reverse direction
headed HOME.

*Seattle to D.C.*
*February-August 1976*

# Pejuta / Red Road

First time was Winnebago way
on the land of road man
Ruben Snake.

Shaking rattles
water drum
sum up the sacrament
center of the altar
on that
crescent half-a-moon

where flaming arrows
from the coals
sear the soul
of born-again heathen
headed East
providing protection
prayers for the Trail
honor blankets
rainbow splashed
(1st) Eagle Feather
finds us
waiting for the Morning Star
to bless us and our feast of
Water
      Berries
           Pemmican
& Corn

*Trail of Self-Determination*
*1976, Winnebago, Nebraska*

# Elegy on the Death of two Indian Women

*for Norma & Billy Franks*
*in memory of Maureen & Ca-Ba-Qhud*


Through winding woods
of warrior Leschi
humbly we accompany
strong gone Woman/
child embracing own
innocent Child woman
to final resting place
in Mother Earth.

"Their memory,
Uncle Billy,
will forever make us
strong".

By sacred sweat lodge
on the brushy banks of
the Nisqually River
copper-contaminated rage
at other wars that here were waged.
We talk of visions & victories
while Valerie's spirit presence
brings energies necessary
for fishing one more day.
Thundering voices from Midwestern plains
soulful strains from the tundra mains
in the land of killer whales
blend together in a harmony
that unites.

Rites postponed in due respect
to varying tribal customs/ways.
And still, tomorrow
as today, defending fishing nets,
we shall be One.

Raza Love & Solidarity
helps ease the hurt somewhat
feasting eases and pleases
tribal relatives traveling
from far & distant ground.
"Round Grandpa Fire
we stood
while Northwest wood crackled
clothing us with warmth
to complement the blessings
of a chilling early Autumn
September sprinkling rain.
And so the tender short-lived
womanchild of sparkling
dimpled smiles
gave life to smiling childwoman
of the too-few-summers
bidding us with brilliant eyes
to simply care.

And so they left us, dear Norma
on journey long
to chart new paths
unknown as yet to us.
Somehow it seems, or so our hearts dictate,
that in their passing to the spirit world
staying with us for a while
they left us with a gift
the giving of ourselves
our future selves.

A young & tender
only brother
warrior standing tall
We call upon him Sugar manchild of the wild
show us the way to strength/by lengthening the will
instilling us with loving
niece & sister
mighty fighting fisherwomen spirit
of Nisqually Valley's
Chief Leschi.
Finally there is another
husband/father
Dunston
brother to us all
departs
to shed his tears
in Northwest Territories
with the clan.
As we leave you to your peace
we remember fishing wars,
defending the nets,
the river in flames,
that as long as the river runs
there are no goodbyes.

*after the Trail of Self-Determination*
*Frank's Landing, Washington*
*Summer of 1977*

# Survival Song

In
fur-lined fascination
    petite sized
fleeting fox
     summer camper!
scampers across
crisscrosses
S
  P
 I
R
  A
    Ling road
leading down
to Grandma George's Beach.

Reaching out to
    meet 'n' greet
(by touching with the eyes)
this instant flash of
    fiery red-pelt radiance
emanating natural
        Native
          magic
somehow makes
    clam digging
      easier
(for indians)
    on this day.

*Suquamish Reservation*
*November 25, 1977*

# Campfire Conversations

The Elders say:

Chiefs Kitsap & Leschi
roamed Northern woods together
hunting/fishing in the
"usual and accustomed" ground
'round Puget Sound
Salish peoples paddled
carved Cedar tree
canoes visiting
Puyallup/Nisqually
Relatives to the South.


The Elders say:

S'Klallam Nation
once was ONE
will be again
instead of three
(Port Gamble/Jamestown/Lower Elwha)
bands dispersed
burned down encampments
clam beds destroyed
then came the plague.

That's what the Elders say . . .

*Suquamish*
*1977*

29

# Medicine Feasting

On this peninsula
we talk well
of our chiefs:
Soft-spoken Sealth,
grave sited in prayer...
in Suquamish
and as we drive past the Point
rebel howls for
kitsap "Black Chief" of the wild
and his bones
never found by the mob.
Robbers of resources return
bearing gifts of missiles
surrounding reservation ground
becoming concentration camp.

Dampened spirit/
lives a-shatter
seeking his/her source
return to beginning
ceremonies experienced alone
seedlings not sown
showing the way
to be Free,
wonderin' if it will ever be
like that year on Black Lake
and the poems written in peace.

It was a time of rememorings
(lest we forget)
diggin' clams on Grandma's Beach

she forever the teacher
to family gathered
in clambake reunion
communion with the tides
warm waves of welcome
approaching whaling season
and springtime melting
of the snows.

*Suquamish – 1977*

31

# Peltier I

*(LIFE SENTENCES*
  *– 2 of them –*
*is what Peltier's got).*


Mientras
past (persistent)
parranda partners
siempre unbelieving
weaving of
Chongo Rojo/Indigena
as warrior trenzas
wrapped in Red
further complex
futile reuniones
Quizas!
not meant to be.

And so WE
aqui en Milwaukee snows
show support for
"Stick-Standing Man"
preso politico
standing trial
while
personas encountered en
previous (un)poetic lives
viven oblivious
de lo obvious
burla
poetas don't grace
covers of
Time

still being done by the BRO.
Sisters carry on the struggle
Turtle Woman awakening
from sleep ... rest
dreamsmiles
before the courts convene
and we must
stand in Solidarity
again.

*Milwaukee, Wisconsin*
*Winter 1978*

# Peltier II

Peltier
Sun Dance Man
Warrior/Hunting Man
brings singing
buffalo
          (penetrating sting)
to shatter
babylonian madness
sadness in the song
Crow Dog
          White Coyote
brings thundering rains
conjures
whispering waters
of
ana mae r
rememorings
"i'll speak with you through the rain."

The Deer
Stood
rooted in his ways
Warriors three
before
the court of
monarchy
tribunal would suppress them
Dressed in prison grey
while
relatives
brighten dull courtroom

all in "colors"
in the traditional mode
plus jail cell matrimony.

Bobby's spirit left
dangling in the dungeon.
Stencils over urban sprawl call.
From the Northwest
"The Fastest Spray can artist"
comes
to test
graffitti gardens
doing dwelling decoration
of the slums.
Eagle feathers come to those who wait ...
and work ...

*Los Angeles*
*Lompoc Escape Trial*
*Fall 1979*

# Prayer for a Newborn

*for Ha'kwa'stobsh*

Raccoon,
      spooning through
weeks-long garbage
on smokeshop cabin
front porch,
brings on
good feelings.

Blue Jays do breakfast
by kitchen-sink window
fry bread
– today's portion of meal –
honoring our dead
as flying smiles
& soaring souls
      heed heartsong
of elders and all:
"For those generations gone before us…,
      for the generations yet unborn."
Inside
mind/heart/souls
Eagle wings/fluttering feathers
Medicine Man fans
auras in good faith.
Some die, so others live,
that's how it gots to be.
All of us must struggle,
so that someone may be free.
Because it's good to be alive
we ask our granpas & granmas

to walk 'n' talk with you.
We welcome you,
Red Cedar Man.
Hau!

*Suquamish, Washington*
*1978*

# De-Urban-I-Zation Blues

Leaving the reservation
under full moon night
ferry ride into Seattle
face off conscience-less council
members continue to sell out
humble community folks
make jokes about no bucks
for viable energy force
land base for the landless
while dynamic designers
resign our own through dialectics
to an unrelenting struggle
for survival's sake.
Anxiety gnaws
at poetic/political craw
as Queen City skyline
comprised of strangling structures
grows in metal/glass/concrete
dimensions, there is a feeling
of constriction
– faint glimmer of prisons past –

– *Seattle, Washington*
*1978*

38

# Returning to the Rez

Returning to the rez
missing 2 boats in the process
choppy Elliot Bay waters
beat turbulent tattoos
on massive marine vessel
that should, by rights
belong in Duwamish hands
banning Washington state ferry
would be okay
owing a buck seventy
'leventy cents & bouncing checks
wrecking passive nerves.
Just goes to show
you can't trust banks
or cranks with 39 dollars
sixty seven cents.
Gently, sea cradling lull
soothing/relaxing
psyche taxed
and long-polluted
as we approach
island rich in
Native Cultures
poor in
bourgeois overflow.

                    – *Suquamish*
                    *1978*

# Suquamish Summer

*to my typewriter*
*(after the "splitting of the sheets")*

hello,
loyal and faith
fully waiting
Companion.
The lonesome traveler is back,
jack!
And I don't mean
Kerouac.
Back from desolate
& depressing year-long
haunting & hurting journey
trek to demon lands.
Sands of TIME
don't ease no PAIN,
thassa whole lotta shit!
And rain, at this point
in time
only makes matters worse.
Thanx a lot.
What started all of this
dilemma/mess
jes' in case
sumbody asks.
Was premature attempts
to alter/change
traditionally-conditioned
reservation humanscape.
The need to heed
(which really never happened,

due to everything else ...)
the mesmerizing music of the muse.
Use-to-be
"families"
so
    long.
Strong feeling of the blues
over d-urban-I
Zing! went the string
of the heart
as if mowed down
by blade of
recently arrived
mountain-cane machete.
Political poets
unable to counter
drunken put-downs
ridicule by the "Bluds."


It's raining on the Rez
stains of coffee/beer/
tears of loneliness
and who knows what all else
become the bursting stars
adorning scars
of crumpled paper
ragged/jagged fragments
bits 'n' pieces
of Suquamish summers
solace . . . life.
Wife off to make the bread
bring bacon home
to starving (for love & affection)
artist/husband
who can be.

See proud Indian Woman/Strength
standing by the highway
hitchhiking to the land of madness
& stench.
Wrenching his "unnurtured"
body/hulk
from sagging sofa-bed
POWERless manCHILD
wildly digs
clawing fingernails
into windowsill
crying still
all over again
41 years later
waves at mama
going out into the world
until she's
outta sight!
Quite a role-reversal
the elders just never understood.
That doing no good
for (tattooed) relationships
thoroughly strained.
Drained
(like sap from maple trees)
of all love & emotions
as gestures & notions
came to portray
nay-saying
what was left
of bereft love affair
gone awry.

And so the story goes:
that once upon a time

there was a lonely house
and in it sat a man, alone.
By the side of a lonely road
stood a woman, alone,
headed for a city
crowded with loneliness.
That the road to the ferry
which led to that city
became ever-widening gap
full of the emptiness
neither could fill.
Killing time before it kill you
(or whatever else it do)
filling notebooks/journals
with cryptic message scrawls
to no one in particular
and of no real consequence
is how this year was wasted...spent!
Bent now (perhaps too late)
on patching up/repairing
so-to-speak
favorite Mexican earthenware
pot not totally complete
shattered shards missing
like the links missing
on handcuff hung in souvenir.
Like missing someone
who's not here.
Fearfully attempt
to reconstruct harmoniously
git-in-toon music
made under an August moon
so long ago.
O' to get past vastness
of a year unclaimed.

Maimed a bit
in the process
but shit,
what the heck!
So the fireworks are all over
the storm sub...sides, re-activates
generating ocean motions
as the tide goes in...and out...
on Agate pass.
Last night at ebbing tide
sirens sang:
"mama's got a brand new ride!"
Warriors weary pray for peace
a chance in the sun.
Fun day for chasing spiders
outta the house
sweeping cobwebs from the walls
halls full of dead memories
living faces fuzzily engraved
etched in the word maze
of surrounding habitat.
Fat with 10 gees in the kitty
(rather than in the titty, this time)
they's s'posed to be happy
pity they not, due to ain't got.
Monty-is-car-low, jim!
Brimming with (dumb) joy
boy booted in the butt
end of joke, folks,
as someone else cruises
in bleeding maroon
down misty city streets
with the lady of the coral stones.
With nothing left but relatives
in distant lands unseen
keen senses (long dormant)

stir lazily with signs of
LIFE.
And so,
returning to the solace
of you, Blue
Mechanical Mistress
engager in techno-trysts
with poets perturbed
disturbing lethargic sleep
thoughts leaping
profess to tell you all.
Falling stars appeared that night
as clustering bees swarmed about
coveting honey.
Knowing you'd be here
secure in Minnesota blanket warmth
(protection from the dust)
just seemed reassuring
enough
to
    say
        hello.


*S'Klallam Nation*
*Port Madison Reservation, Washington*
*July 13, 1978*

## Cedar Woman Poem

Walking on our way
to confront
wicked B.I.A.
cutting slack
to the go-down in Oglala
yellow was the shawl
that somewhat wrapt your
dancing/prancing nipples
creating sensuous ripples
in my soul.
Late summer in Suquamish
Chief Seattle days
clam digging with "the boys"
family again.

Trail of Self-Determination
morning in Nebraska
Black Dog runs the sweat
as we sing bear songs
chanting to Chichayo
Indio/Mejicano
political prisoners
Dennis & Chacón.
Meanwhile
making love in
vintage command car
turned
communications van,
bedroom on wheels.

Camping out in Pittsburgh
a pretty poet comes to call
placing poems all over me
and you swear she had
her boobs up in my face.

Then came the season
of the "roaring guns"
shattering peaceful retreat
where we read poems
on the banks of Skookum Creek.

Years later
I pass old & familiar spots
headed towards another
fishing battle
on Hupa lands.

*Hupa Reservation*
*Humboldt County, Ca.*
*1979*

## Song of a Sad Lover

After you left
folks on the rez
couldn't understand
my pain
as you suffered
with me.

People also
thought it strange
that we could talk
and share our hurts
revealing open wounds
of love no longer there.

Sharing each other's energies
and love intense
with one and all in
other moments more serene.

We'd loved hard
amid jazz sounds
and drums from
tribal mounds.

Holidays in the city
get somewhat rough
down moments/thoughts depressed
clam digging comes to mind
then off to hustle urban dollar bills.

And even now
sunday morning rides
up Beacon Hill
Jazz ballads
somehow remind me
of
you.

*Seattle, Washington*
*1979*

49

# Sad Day in the Village

The boys would ask
as we sat on the "slab"
by the bay,
"How does it feel?"
after she of the canoe people
and me, split the sheets.

And I, wanting
to let them know
it hurt, responded
in "guy talk" –
not too poetically, I might add.

"It was like – draggin'
your hemmorhoids on a
concrete sidewalk of a
hot August day in Tejas."

I mean, what could i say
about that day full
of sadness and pain?
Except that it was raining
on the island
when we went away.

*Suquamish, Washington*
*1979*

# Casualties of War

*(for John Trudell)*

Foreign flags in flames
in house of great white father.
Across the country in Shoshone
land by Wild Horse Reservoir
in the Valley of the Ducks
as if in vengeance,
home becomes funeral pyre
for relatives young and old.


Through raging winds
and flurries of fresh-fallen snows
cries in unison of anger/sorrow
soothed by Oglala Lakota
pipe-woman smoke.


Sweet grass from the Plains
round desert & flat northwest
cedar for smudging
Sacred Tipi/Meta Tantay medicine
prepare the way.


From all the four directions
of the sacred Turtle's back we came
for the burial of our own.

And we humbly
(in two traditions)
delivered our relations
to the warm womb
of Mother the Earth.

*Duck Valley Reservation*
*Owyhee, Nevada*
*February 1979*

# Canada Poem

Blustery
cold
loneliness
of
Lake Ontario
freeze formed
icy lace along
the outer edges
of my heart.

The biting wind
wove tapestries
upon your face
as we searched
for the place
of comfort
by
Ceremonial fires
'neath spires of love
as we kissed
          in the mist
of a turbulent
Toronto night.

Climbing (unknown) darkened heights
no lights! those winter nights
of love
begetting
Spring.

Bells ring
singing we heard in the distance,
hear?
Tears flow freely without fear
as we stand
demanding sovereignty
for the
Quebecois!
Shouts of Justice! from Jamaica Town
frown on cop runs invading their homes
gun down Albert Johnson
while postal workers
threatened with jobs/call for STRIKE!
in Thunder Bay
on a day when
          the "commies" showed
NO support!
Reed Paper Mills
pumps poison
into fishing water systems
mercury spills make victims
of fish and fisher people
MINIMATA hits the rez
diseased natives/toxically complete
do the Cat's dance
on the White Dog reserve.

I didn't meet any drunken indians
in Ontario province, I say
(which doesn't mean there weren't any)
maybe 'cause I wasn't drunk myself.
Turtle Woman weeps
as we remember
brothers choking
sisters soaking
all embalmed in alcohol

along First Avenue
Seattle/original skid road
where loads of native
victory visions & dynamic dreams
lay scattered
shattered like so many bottles
of (Red Nation-robbing)
WHITE
        Port wine
conjured up by
Ojibwa/Meshica
third eyes
in those evanescent,
fleeting moments
of a slowly fading
northern sun.

*Toronto, Ontario Canada*
*March 1980*

# Prayer upon a Warrior's Return

Tunkashila,
Grandfather of all grandfathers,
Kaiya,
ancestral grandmother,
thank you for this day.
For bringing us together
once again
to be of one heart . . . of one mind,
we thank you.

We ask that you bring
"good medicine"
to all our relations
those met/then left behind,
a part of us, now
wrapped in woodland warmth.
For Wandering Spirit's
Little People,
we pray.
For Turtle Woman/companion
Son/Ta-wa-sawa-ka,
for everyone here . . . within
    this sacred circle . . .
PEACE.
Give us the strength to be humble,
Grandfather.
Grandmother, give us the strength
to urge one another to rest,
for our work will be
both long and hard.

Grandfather,
grant us who are weak
the will to continue fulfilling
instilling desires/fanning the fires
of our kind to be Free.

For wisdom we ask,
to understand evil forces
with illusions of power
tools of repression
and weapons of war;
those who would keep us
contain us from being
and living (in reality)
a Red Nationhood.

Good feelings
for our sisters/
brothers in the cage of iron
behind stone walls
in the hospitals, foster homes, on alcohol.

For the elders,
the young ones, the "ruggies."
For our relatives
in the woods and in the sky,
in the waters, on the earth.
For the grand Sun . . .
for the grand Moon,
guiding lights,
fighting women of our people
Life-giving force,
we pray.
For patience/endurance to wage further battles.

For a better world,
more humane . . . less insane
and more sharing,
grandmother/grandfather.

All of these things
we ask in your name;
Hau!
Mitakuye Oyasin.

*Toronto, Ontario Canada*
*March 5 & 6, 1980*

# Cultural Exchange

In solid Southwest
Northwest inner weavings
Leroy would say –
attempting to lure
Ramona (the one from tejas)
to dip in the net
for skein full
of fresh salmon eggs –

"C'mon, gal,
just drop sac into pan
of simmering (not boiling) water,
slice of onion,
salt and pepper;
a wedge of lemon if you like."

"No caviar here, dear
ain't got no roe to go.
Just a simple ind'n meal
that tastes almost like
your red soup 'Menoodle' does
back home."

*Frank's Landing, Washington*
*1981*

# Lakota Road Journals

Traditional elder
LoudHawk
does symbolic gesture
to unheeding heads
of state,
"A hundred horses
for the return of our
brother."

Silver Bullet caravan
secures the route
to Wind Cave
reclamation of Lakota
Paha Sahpa (eh sahpa)
sacred earth.

*June 29, 1981*

Elijah Whirlwind Horse
was providing the cow
(promised since April!)
for Yellow Thunder Camp.

Literally truckin' down
to Wanblee
then, back to the Knee
be in Pine Ridge
by tomorrow.

Sorrow for the Brave
graveside ceremonies
in language yet untainted
by wily Wasi'chu ways.

Eagle Claw Warrior says:
"Between the Badlands' beauty
and the final change of worlds,
there MUST be peace."

*Wanblee to Pine Ridge Rez*
*July 2, 1981*

# After the Memorial

On Mount Rushmore
stone faces loom
in gloomy grey
across Lakota
holy landscape.

On far side of the hills
Chief Crazy Horse emerges
adding to eh sahpa grace
in all her radiant colors,

Racing outta' Rapid
with newsletter, posters
and gas money for the road.

Arriving on time to witness
Oglalas voting
unanimously to stay
paving the way to
Wind Cave/Custer, S.D.

Custer, sight of rights denied
(both mineral and aboriginal)
to those so long ago
abused.

Amused elder voice of
Stanley Looking Elk says,
"Welcome to Crazy Horse camp,
my relatives, you are here."

*Wind Cave, South Dakota*
*July 8, 1981*

# Ahbleza

AHBLEZA!
  blazin'
burnin' the blues away
swaying sounds
sooth pounding
minds of Marion/
Attica atrocities.
Reservation Rock
appeals to ally
relatives around the
globe.
Blue Mahto
(free from Franklin Street)
mobilizes musical support
& solidarity
for Red Nations/
Natural people
to survive.
Striving for that Inter/
National
connect.
Commending mutual
Respect.

*White Earth Reservation*
*Minnesota*
*1981*

## Umbrellas After the Rain

I'd returned
to pack up memories left scattered
shattered and peeling
(almost with no feeling)
tattered extensions off the wall.

Coffee call comes through
early a.m. conversations
suppressing sensations
of a time before.

I'd returned
with all our joys
and pains contained
within the pages of a book.

Looking to please
and tease you/
share with you
what you always referred to
(things after the fact)
as "umbrellas after the rain."

Misty was the morning
drizzle muffled moments
tense/sadness
then gladness release.

New visions verbalized
of Southern relations

of sacred cactus circle
Shaman energy source.

Talk of home at last
of eras past
"gone and get you"
end of the exile
mending the hoop
and the
Indian woman of the South
who dances barefoot
upon the stones.

We kissed, you left
having expressed
some regret.
Doorbell rings
you re-enter
"what a way to say goodbye."

Entire pack of publications
drop in all directions.
Embracing we cry.
Trying to be cool,
I almost wanted/
needed to say...
can't we...?
But you were late for work
our coffee cups were dry
and so was I.

I think of you
Cedar Woman
as I caress the
blue/orange
floral beaded buckskin

pouch from Mohawk lands
which carries braided
sweet grass and a lock
of your medicined hair.

*Seattle, Washington*
*June 13, 1982*

# Bay Area Breather

She carries a flute
and a brush
faintly painting
soothing sounds
musical murals
sing from wailing walls
assail the colony.

Turtles
and spinning Frida Kahlo
mandalas surround the warrior
"for protection," she assures.
After a night of much needed
respite from the road
awakening to neon
unnatural lights
sip on cool horchata drink
thinking of another ind'n;
Maira, walking the streets
of Managua, child in one arm
AK-47 in the other.

Today words come
in form of kites
of native essence
"the prince of peace
is gone." Nina sings
bringing Northwest winds
closer to us

cultures on canvas
flute serenades
and our work
for the captive in the cage.


*San Francisco*
*January 1982*

## The Invitation

Grandma Jumping Bull...
with a hundred years wisdom
upon her back
says it's lonesome in the city.
"ah'm lonely for my place,
ah wanna go home".

Walking out the door
she stops
leans on her equally aged,
carved & cut-glass beaded
walking stick,
turns around
looks back at us
and says:
"when you AIM boys comin' to mah land?"

In a matter of hours, Grandma,
in a matter of hours...
to cleanse ourselves
from city sludge
smudged all over our souls.

*(after Rapid City)*
*Pine Ridge Reservation*
*Oglala, South Dakota*
*June 21, 1982*

# Court 'n' Cave Times

Slow-walk through brilliant Autumn woods
far from snowbound Northern Reserves

vows made somewhat formally
inside Midwestern caves escaping
tingling October rains, promising

to keep their LOVE secret —
Safely
Protected — like so many burnished
leaves pressed in a book —
between the lines and verses
of their most intimate
& sacred
poems.

*St. Louis, Missouri*
*1986*

# Soul Search 'n' Hill Country Woods

Visits with the elements had long diminished
when healing was in order for the clan
fluttering feathers/sacred spotted hawk
begins cleansing
of injured hearts become the stones
bones rattled
shattered the onyx night
when turtles paired
a further confirmation
laying on a log/feet in the water
at evening tide
touched by the radiant
singeing
of a setting Sun.

*St. Louis, Missouri*
*1986*

# Feel Good Song

*(in the Dineh way)*

Knowledge is beginning.
Knowledge has no end.
Knowledge is forever.
Knowledge is living.

Live and learn.
Live and teach.
Live to know.
Live to give.
Knowledge is beginning.

Walk and you will know.
Walk and Be.
Walk in harmony.
Walk in/to spirit worlds.
Knowledge has no end.

Stay busy.
Stay strong.
Stay honest.
Stay rested.
Knowledge is forever.

Talk to comfort.
Talk to honor.
Talk of injustice.
Talk for healing.
Knowledge is living

Knowledge is living.
Knowledge is forever.
Knowledge has no end.
Knowledge is beginning.

*Big Mountain, Arizona*
*November 16, 1987*

## Pueblo Murals

Pueblo murals
eagle dancers
soar above
adobe walls.
Falling rains
(whisperings of Ana Mae)
gain ground
escort out of town
call to the falcon
hawk.
In the hustle & bustle
of an Albuquerque
springtime
headed toward
blue clouds of Hopi land
and final visit with
saguaro spirits
on Roberto's rez.

Entering desert
pouches couch
the woman who weaves
tranquility within the storm
tapestries speak of turtles
night of narrative notations
alleviate somewhat
mind/spirit/body/soul
relief, time to get away
to assess & survey
the turbulence of the times.

*T'ohono O'odham Nation*
*Sells, Arizona, 1987*

74

# High Flying Eagle

High! / Flying
sacred eagle
gracefully gliding
(almost hiding)
over pastel heavens

Much-
        Needed Medicine
for Warriors weary
from Battling the Beast.
Protection ENsured
making struggles bearable

"Staying on Top of Things"

Understanding life's experiences
In thankfulness and prayer
in total resistance
listening to that other voice
receiving message loud and clear
"Remember who you really are!"

Sacred circle formed
by pair of fighting fish
manifesting cycles
of the integration
between earth & sky
as (red) salmon
live to spawn
and spawn again
reaching that eternal
High!

*Texas Hill Country*
*October 18, 1988*

## About Invasion and Conquest

*composed during the quincentenary
monopoem literary circle*

They came with disrespectful feet
trampling sacred soil
strangers lacking color,
as if unkissed by the Sun.
Bearing cutlass and cross,
grossly they stepped on our land
to be honored with gifting
as guests at the feast.
But greedy for gold
tobacco offerings were considered primitive
then placed among the other
fruits ripe for plucking,
sucking Native resources
to be peddled in the market place
before the queen.
As the pillage and plunder continued,
a young Taino asked: "Who will be left
to tell of what happened to us, Grandfather?"
The elder replies: "Among those who survive,
there will be poets to recount
that which happened to us."
Ay, cristobal colón ...! y que colón!
Long tail that left doors open
for the other clowns/cortes and the boys,
clumsily rattling sabre and sword
lording over indio sharing customs
clad in tin costumes Metallica never would claim.
Maiming Warrior Women,
stripping of the chieftains,

they proceeded to cut down our flowers
tried to silence our songs.

DIScovery in what god's name???
"Who will live to tell  of what happened to us,
Grandmother?" a young Mexica asked.
La Anciana responds: "Among the survivors
there will be poets, they will relate
that which happened to us."
Six generations later, after the bison is (almost) gone
ravaged Mother Earth, by force produces
matter that turns into bombs,
belching poison taints the waters,
kills the plants, pollutes the skies –
contaminates communities
victims of toxic chemical wars.

And today ... and today ... and today,
when 500-plus winters have passed,
among the survivors
are poets
sitting in circle
telling the stories
of peoples in struggle
in total
    Resistencia
and with plena
Dignidad!

*International Day of Solidarity*
*with Indigenous People*
*Austin, Texas*
*October 10, 1992*

# Clouds over the Peak at Dawn

Like fluffy puffs
of cotton candy
smoothly, ever-so-slowly
spinning their charm
like arms of warm softness
sliding down
over and around
a chocolate and vanilla
ice cream cone.

*Windcall Retreat*
*in "The Valley of the Flowers"*
*Belgrade, Montana*
*June 26, 1996*

# Offering to Marsha

Poetry:
Turtle spirits
with lizard medicine.

Sacred sweet grass to smudge your path
accompany you
along that Blue Road
on your voyage
to the other place.

To you,
comrade/sister
my relative
of two spirit
Choctaw/Chicanindia
energicni
I honor you
today
as you take your place
beside
the mother of the universe.

To you, Marsha Morning Gomez
I bring this humble
offering, a gift
braided with love.
What soul of a woman!
Here is my heart.

*Austin, Texas*
*February 6, 1999*

# About the Author

Raúl R. Salinas was born in San Antonio, Texas, on St. Patrick's Day in 1934. He grew up in La Loma, an eastside barrio of Austin. Salinas first encountered the blues and jazz that would shape his inner rhythms for the rest of his life in the clubs of Austin. Mexican corridos and other traditional music filled the barrio, making for a rich cultural soup. Similarly, the mixture of Black English, school English (enforced), Texas Spanish, Spanish border radio, all merged to form the linguistic environment from which Salinas's poetic idiom would evolve.

In 1952, Salinas dropped out of school to join the Pachuco equivalent of the newly christened "Beat Generation," so he headed west to see what there was to see – and to work in the fruit orchards of California. The police being what they were at the time, it was easy for a footloose hipster Chicano from Texas to fall prey to a sting operation. In 1957, he was sent to Soledad State Penitentiary, where he began writing. Here he began to bring together the disparate elements of his life and times – the West Coast avant garde and his Tejano heritage, the freedom of Beat literature and revisionist rigors of a young poet still unsure of his abilities. Released from Soledad in 1959, he was busted in Texas in 1961 and sent to Huntsville State Prison on drug-related charges. There he began writing a jazz column for the prison newspaper, *The Echo*. One of his essays, "So Much Mystery, So Much Misunderstanding," made it to the outside and was published in the *Beaumont Enterprise* in 1964. Released in 1965, he was busted again in 1967. This time he was sent to Leavenworth.

The federal penitentiary proved to be a unique educational institution. Here Salinas met several "organic intellectuals" and political prisoners whose reading matter included radical publications like *The Militant*, *Grito del Norte*, and *The Guardian*, as well as the works of Che Guevara, Amilcar Cabral, and other writers involved with Third World revolutionary ideologies. Salinas became acutely aware of the continuing oppression of Native Americans, the struggle for Puerto Rican independence, and the racism and classism endemic to the Anglo-American power structure. A multiracial cadre of prisoners banded together to demand improved educational opportunities, which resulted in a class taught by Francisco Ruíz entitled "The Cultural History of the Southwest." Thus did Salinas encounter the radical Chicano politics of the time. The group of prisoner-students began producing a newspaper, *Aztlan de Leavenworth*. In the first issue, Salinas's poem "Un trip through the mind jail" first appeared. If there is a Chicano "Howl," it is "Un trip." The poem was circulated as a loose sheaf of mimeographed pages before it appeared in the poet's now-legendary chapbook, *Viaje/Trip* (Hellcoal, 1973). It appeared again in his 1980 collection of poems, *Un Trip through the Mind Jail y Otras Excursiones*.

Prison officials shut down *Aztlan de Leavenworth* after six issues, due to its political content, and identified Salinas as a malcontent troublemaker. Along with other politically radical prisoners from all over the U.S., Salinas was transferred to the federal penitentiary in Marion, Illinios. Salinas' letters to the mainstream press were important in drawing attention to prison conditions and the violation of prisoner rights. They also drew attention to his own case, and in November 1972, Salinas was released, in part due to a campaign mounted by students and faculty at the University of Washington in Seattle.

After this 15-year rollercoaster ride through the American correctional system, Salinas emerged "a whole lot better hombre than the youth who first entered the joint," as he puts it. Like his pinto-poet peers, Ricardo Sánchez and Jimmy Santiago Baca, Salinas emerged as a well-read, highly committed activist poet.

Conscious of both his Native American and Chicano roots, Salinas spent the next ten years working closely with AIM, the American Indian Movement. This period of his life is described by Professor Louis Mendoza in his introduction to *Indio Trails*. As Salinas wrote in "Amorindio," he found the same demands for human rights and for land rights "from Pine Ridge to Chiapas/del barrio de la Loma/a la selva

Lacandona." This sense of solidarity among all the indige-
nous peoples of the Americas is the defining characteristic of
Salinas' polemic against the status quo. It is no surprise that
his poetics fuse his own Chicano-Indigenous roots, Third
World liberation ideologies, and Beat poetry, which emulat-
ed jazz in its fusion of political, cultural and social elements
and styles.

Since the mid-1980s, Salinas has run a bookstore,
Resistencia Books, and a small press, Red Salmon, in Austin.
He has done extensive work with gang intervention and rec-
onciliation across the country. He remains an indefatigable
advocate for prisoner rights around the globe.

Salinas's second full-length collection of poems, *East of
the Freeway*, was published in 1996. Recently, Salinas has
produced several CDs of his work, accompanied by every-
thing from the Pacific surf to native drums to cool jazz to
experimental solo baritone sax. These include *Los Many
Mundos of raúlrsalinas* (Calaca Press, 2000), *Beyond the
Beaten Path* (Red Salmon, 2002), and *Red Arc: A call for lib-
eración con salsa y cool* (Wings, 2005).

*Indio Trails* is a more reflective work, a poetic chronicle
of the poet's physical, intellectual and spiritual odyssey into
his indigenous roots, and a celebration of survival:

And today ... and today ... and today,
when 500-plus winters have passed,
among the survivors
are poets
sitting in circle
telling the stories
of peoples in struggle
in total
    Resistencia
and with plena
Dignidad!

                       – *con respeto*, B.M.

Wings Press was founded in 1975 by Joanie Whitebird and Joseph F. Lomax as "an informal association of artists and cultural mythologists dedicated to the preservation of the literature of the nation of Texas." The publisher /editor since 1995, Bryce Milligan is honored to carry on and expand that mission to include the finest in American writing. To that end, we at Wings Press publish multicultural books, chapbooks, CDs and broadsides that enlighten the human spirit and enliven the mind. We know well that writing is a transformational art form capable of changing the world by allowing us to glimpse something of each other's souls.

Wings Press uses as much recycled material as possible, from the paper on which the books are printed to the boxes in which they are shipped.

## *Colophon*

This first edition of *Indio Trails*, by raúlrsalinas, has been printed on 70 pound paper containing fifty percent recycled fiber. The text has been set in a contemporary version of Classic Bodoni. The font was originally designed by 18th century Italian punchcutter and typographer Giambattista Bodoni, press director for the Duke of Parma. Titles and initial capitals have been set in Cochin. All Wings Press books are designed and produced by Bryce Milligan.

Our complete catalogue is available at

www.wingspress.com

Wings Press and Raúlrsalinas gratefully acknowledge the City of Austin Cultural Arts Division, for a generous grant, which made possible the publication of *Indio Trails*.

**Cultural Arts
Division**